Ricky Dee
Scribbles & Scratches

Brooke Dyson
Layout & Design

For Elias and Ada
my favorite Cubs

Kalos Design
2014
absolutelyunprofessional.com

© 2014 Produced and Published by Kalos Design
All rights reserved. This book or any portion thereof may not be reproduced or used in any manner whatsoever without the express written permission of the publisher except for the use of brief quotations in a book review or scholarly journal.

First Printing: 2014
ISBN 978-0-9914581-0-3
Kalos Design
114 W. Prospect St.
Wadsworth, OH 44281

Comic Book font from Pixel Sagas Freeware Fonts EULA

Find Bearly Dad updates and more:
    absolutelyunprofessional.com

Dear Journal:

As the Great Slambino once said, "A little healthy Rumblin' saves from a lot of Grumblin'."

That is, a little rumble with the cubs, a little play, a little direction, a little discipline each day goes a long way in modeling and passing on love and respect... so Let's Rumble!

Enjoy,
BEARLY DAD

Now listen closely. I'm only going to say this once.

Go on.

No biting, pinching or pulling hair. Stay out of the arm pits, off the gully and on the ground. We're not animals so let's keep it clean...I've got a full day of school ahead of me tomorrow.

Well then **Wembleton** my boy, let's rumble.

Ugh...Hummph...Would you PLEASE roll-over BEARLY DAD!

Oh, if only I could my boy. Now listen up. This move is a long-standing tradition. In fact, it's been a family secret handed down from ages past and one day you'll be a Dead Rabbit too, son. Take note of the realistic twitch in my hind quarters.

One thing BEARLY DAD. My rules state that you MUST keep your feet on the ground.

...He circles below the surface of the deep. Gathering speed he leaps toward the heavens, untethered from the saltwater. Light as a butterfly yet big as a whale. Soaring high above the small, innocent seagull below. He begins his descent...

INCOMING!

batter-UP!

RRRRRRR...MUST UPROOT THE MEAN, SILLY, STINKY, OLD TREE.

THIS HAS BEEN A FAMILY FAVORITE FOR CENTURIES WEMBLETON MY BOY. SEE HOW MY FEET BECOME ONE WITH THE GROUND, JUST AS YOUR RULES COMMAND. IN FACT, YOUR GRANDFATHER MAY STILL BE PLANTED LIKE THIS IN MY CHILDHOOD HOME...NOW THAT'S COMMITMENT! OH SWEET TRADITION.

RRRRRRRR...CAN I HAVE A CHILL-POP NOW?

Now, when I was a young cub I had to jump high and fast to evade the damage caused by this knee-bending machine of terror.

One thing BEARLY DAD. If it was so painful when you were a cub, why are you now unleashing it's fury upon me?

Tradition son...Tradition.

Awe, how comfy and cute he is all bundled up so tight in his cutey little burrito wrap.

Not cool BEARLY DAD.

I thought it might do you well to rest after that last move my boy. Truly, I had no idea human legs could bend at such angles. You look pretty cozy in there...

Not cool at all.

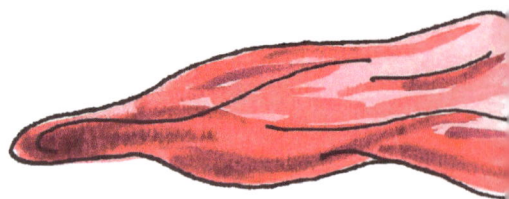

One thing BEARLY DAD. I believe you're blatantly ignoring one of the key Rumblin' rules once again. That said, would you please place my feet back on the ground?

Oh yes, yes, yes of course, though before I do, did I ever tell you about the time I once hung upside down by my feet for nearly a week during the great blizzard?

No, I don't believe so. Was that how you lost your hair? I suppose your hair simply couldn't hold on any longer...
fell out...
abandoned ship...
you're bald.

We're done here.

Not cool son.

I couldn't help it! I was upside down *HAHA*... and my tummy rumbled *HAHAHA*...and *HAHA*...

WHAT DO YOU THINK WEMBLETON? I CALL IT THE CLOSER! A NEW ADDITION TO TRADITION.

I'M BEGINNING TO THINK MY LIST OF RULES IS NOT QUITE AS COMPREHENSIVE AS I'D FIRST THOUGHT.

Bearly dad?

Yes son.

Do you think we could Rumble again tomorrow night before bed?

Sounds like a great plan my boy.

One Thing Bearly dad.

Yes Wembleton.

Well, I think we'll need to clarify some of the rules once again.

Good night son.

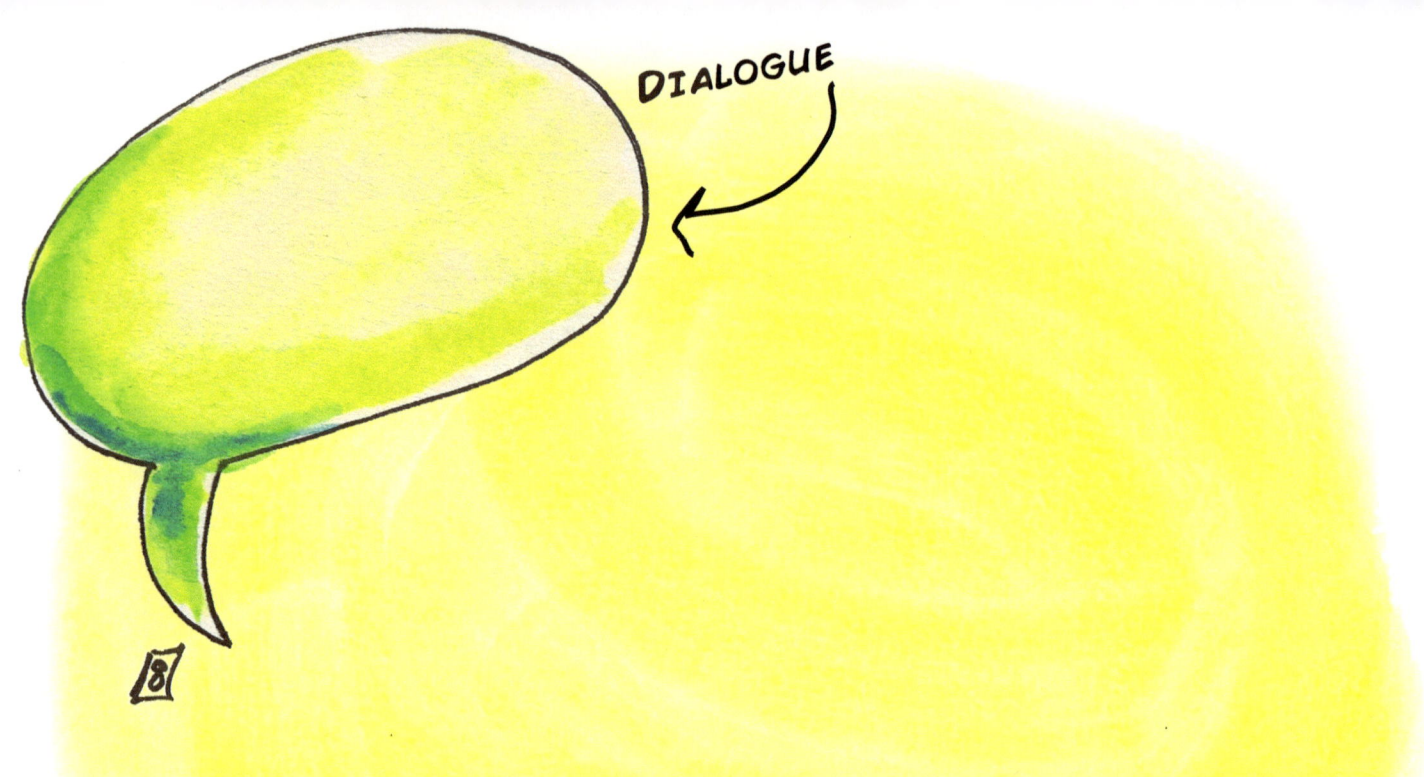

(Record Your Own Rumble Tradition)

Look for the incredible follow-up!
BEARLY DAD: The Untold Tales ...Now Told
'IF I WERE A...'

(UNLESS I CHANGE MY MIND AND TITLE IT SOMETHING ELSE. OR I SUPPOSE I MIGHT SIMPLY SCRAP THE PROJECT ALTOGETHER. I MEAN I'M WINGIN' IT HERE FOLKS! OH, THE PERKS OF BEING MY OWN BOSS.)

www.ingramcontent.com/pod-product-compliance
Lightning Source LLC
Chambersburg PA
CBHW061401090426
42743CB00002B/99